HEART WORK

Published by BooxAi
ISBN: 978-965-578-624-8

Heart Work

Kevin Wright

AUTHOR'S DEDICATION

Heart Work is inspired by my grandmother, Ruby Lee Wright; her presence was poetry. This collection is dedicated to the Black womxn who raised me, loved me, cared for me, and helped me discover my purpose to serve as a voice for the voiceless.

AUTHOR BIO

Kevin was raised in the Historic Westside of Las Vegas, NV, with the love and labor of multiple Black womxn. Born from a lineage of African, Creole, and Indigenous ancestry, he currently serves as a Racial Equity Advocate and Consultant, where he is responsible for serving as a voice for the voiceless. Wright's commitment to racial justice, equity, and inclusion is guided by his approach to dismantling systems rooted in white supremacy while advocating for individuals with historically marginalized identities. After over a decade of ghostwriting, Kevin decided to claim his own voice and thoughts by sharing who he is through the gift of poetry. This would not be possible without the care, guidance, and mentorship of other poets and artists in the Las Vegas community.

Illustrator Bio

Cristina Meraz Garcia is a Mexican-American artist, born in 1993 in Evanston, Illinois, and moved to Las Vegas at a young age with her mother, brother, father, and dog, Osa. She has been drawing since the age of 5. Art has always been such a big part of Cristina's life, starting with inspiration from her older brother, Raul. Cristina began to notice this was a way for her to escape and to focus on drawing to become better every chance she could. Drawing was all Cristina could think about and do; in school, teachers used to take her pens and markers away, and even pencils, because all she would do was find ways to draw either on herself or on things around her. Cristina was inspired by so many things, such as movies, music, photography, love, and traveling to places she'd never seen before. As Cristina got older, life came in fast; she let herself, others, and things get in the way of her fire and her love to make time for art. Later in life, she was able to find that light, with the door still cracked open and never closed. Cristina began to create once again, challenging herself with new ways to make art. She believed in herself enough to start selling custom pieces to people, as well as doing make-up. Meeting some amazing people along the way, Cristina was able to create custom designs for her first client, Legendary Empowerment. While working full-time in the medical field, Cristina also illustrated designs for an educational book titled, "Pearls for Primary Care: Integrating Biochemistry, Physiology, and Clinical Skills To Optimize Outpatient Medicine" by Dr. Michael B. Jacobs. Cristina's goal is to be able to create or to be a part of a creation that is beautiful, moving, and inspiring for herself and for others.

ILLUSTRATOR'S DEDICATION

I'd like to dedicate this publication to the people who saw something in me when I didn't. To the people that gave me opportunities to be a better version of myself. To the people I never get to see again, or enough, but I remember how they impacted my life. My brother, Raul, for starting this fire in me as a kid. My mom, Carmela, and my pops, Raul, for always believing in my talent. Thank you. A special thank you to Kevin for being patient with me, guiding me, believing in me, and having the trust and the opportunity to be alongside him in making this come to life. HEYO!

CMerazArt

Mission Statement: The purpose of my business is to be able to do something that I love and have an outlet for everything that I feel.

Vision Statement: To create custom art pieces that are beautiful, moving, and inspiring. To be the preferred artist for custom creations. To have others be able to visualize themselves in my work.

Illustrator's Note

Each poem has a different style of art because of the different emotions they activate. I aimed to infuse my art with Kevin's vision and poetic style. This project granted me the opportunity to express myself freely, and I hope you enjoy what I created.

Instagram: Cmeraz_art

TikTok: Cmeraz_art

Author's Note

Healing is hard.

Heart Work is a means to stop letting the past go unchecked. It is an opportunity to be face-to-face with the things you thought no longer hurt you. While the poems are written from my lived experiences, I acknowledge these experiences are not mine exclusively. I hope these poems resonate with the reader in a way that reminds them that they are not alone.

Healing is hard.

However, you don't have to do it alone. Heart Work is a reminder that it is okay to ask for help and be vulnerable. It also reminds us to set boundaries, speak our truth responsibly, and let go of the things and people that no longer add value to our lives. This is a moment where we can have the audacity to take back our right and ability to heal.

Healing is hard.

I hope these poems make you feel seen. Everyone's journey looks different, and what matters is that you don't lose sight of the end goal. Heart Work pushes us to be okay with expecting and accepting non-closure. Coming to terms with love, loss, transition, trauma, and many other things is not a cute or quick process. However, waking up each day to be better is a blessing in itself.

Healing is hard.

Yet, we are resilient! Don't forget about your worth and value in this world. Don't discount where you've been, and don't lose sight of where you're going. You are a miracle and a work in progress all at once.

Contents

The Drifter

Maybe I'm here to exist instead of actually live

To exist in a manner where I spread as much light as possible

And then go home to sit in darkness

To break rules

To reframe ideologies

To challenge the norm

To bring about positive change

Only for others to enjoy

I don't want to exist

I want to live

I want to love

I want to be in love

But maybe I don't deserve that

Because it's not my purpose

I've given so much to others

Yet my generosity is

mistaken for harmful intent

It pains me to witness

how one's harm still has power over them

It hurts knowing some can never

understand how much love they deserve

You suffer in silence

You endure much struggle
You encounter so much evil
You ask for happiness
You pray for better

And then you get it
But have no idea what to do with it
You don't wanna lose it
And yet you don't think you can accept it
You figure it's a lose-lose situation
If you accept it, but fuck up, you lose it
And if you let it go, you still lose it

I'm sorry for representing uncertainty for you
My only intention was
to give you what you deserve
and what you asked for
I just wanna live
But it seems like that's not my purpose
So I'll just be here and exist
and watch you accept my gifts
From someone else

Hmm

It took a lot for me to be here

A womxn's peace was interrupted with fear

A man fought to protect his family

His colonizers gave him a choice: the ship or the sea

A fucked up cruise trip traveled to foreign land

A man and womxn struggled to stay together hand in hand

They were stripped of their names and had to learn a distinct trade

This man and womxn were forced to be enslaved

They had children who fought to not be separated

Born into a world where their Blackness triggered hatred

Over a hundred years of ridicule and pain

With freedom on their mind, and liberation to gain

To get away from their colonizers, they had to travel far

If they couldn't find the railroad, they still had the north star

Fast forward through the timeline just a bit

I wish I could share more, but my history wasn't properly documented

A mother decided to take a chance on the west

Her daughter alongside her hoping for the best

The men in their lives phased in and out

They stopped protecting their womxn and went looking for white clout

The daughter, once a girl, grew up very quickly

Then she had her own daughter and the father left her as fast as he fucked her: swiftly

These three womxn lived a life wanting to experience Black joy

Then another surprise came into the mix, a baby Black boy

At the age of 9, he lost his first love

Ruby, you're missed, I know you're watching from above

He grows up quick and is faced with nothing but violence

4 knife wounds, 4 bullet holes, and damaged nerves make him suffer in silence

Eventually, he loses his heart

The ignorance of a drunk driver tore his life apart

He fights to protect his family

While others try to control his destiny

He leaves his home and vacated the nest

Everyone angered by his decision because only they knew what was best

10 years later he comes back to them

He goes back home but his home didn't recognize him

He's a stranger in the community

Having to once again fight people who want to control his destiny

He's his own man

Home reminded him who's a friend and who's just a fan

He relinquishes projected expectations

He lets go of any and all limitations

He is free

He is....me

It took a lot for me to be here

It took a lot for me to be here....with you

Please don't take me for granted

Prodigal Son

I started my life with you

You raised me

You gave me

an upbringing that wasn't the best

But it wasn't your fault

I grew to love you

the same way you loved me

But I wanted something more

Something different

I thought you'd be happy for me

As much as you tried to cheer me on

There was resentment in your eyes

I left

And you thought you had to say goodbye

I would come by to visit every once in a while

But it was never enough for you

What was a weekend getaway for me

was a 3-day gaslighting marathon for you

We became more distant

At first I was only next door

Then I was on the opposite side of the country

You told me I turned my back on you

and to never return

We were on and off for 10 years

Then one day I decided to finally come back

You felt a mixture of emotions

I finally came back to you

But wasn't welcomed with open arms

I noticed much had changed about you

You looked different

you acted different

you had new friends

I noticed you started picking up

toxic habits from your other neighbor

I thought I was coming back to something familiar

Instead, I came back

to slowly fading memories I have of you

There was a time I once called you home

But now I'm just a stranger in the desert

The Garden

Last week, a 6-year old Black boy was arrested

for picking flowers

Specifically tulips

Tulips symbolize perfect and deep love

This 6-year old Black boy was filled with

a perfect and deep love

Just like those tulips

And now it's been taken away

You see, this Black boy was probably filled with

wonder

innocence

and a thirst for experiencing

what the world had to offer

Only he didn't realize some parts of the world

dislike his existence

even though he brought

nothing into this world

except a perfect and deep love

His Blackness should leave people

in awe of his beauty

just like the first sight of a garden in the middle of spring

Imagine if this world looked at that Black boy

the way he looked at those Tulips

I'm sure the world would be different if that was the case

This Black boy, like a rose

should've been cared for

respected

nurtured

and its environment

should've watched him grow

Instead, this Black boy, like weeds

was met with unkindness

judgement

disgust

and removed from it's home

The main difference: weeds are naturally destructive

This Black boy wasn't

This Black boy was filled with

a deep and perfect love

A perfect and deep love

many of you don't deserve

Because you're not worthy of it

Because it scares you

Because it's unconditional

Because it's "different"

Because....it's Black

Last week, a 6-year old Black boy

was arrested for picking flowers

The new headline should instead read

"Last week, the world erased a perfect and deep love"

Little One

It can sometimes be scary

to know that the universe made sure we met

Living separate lives

yet having similar themes

The loss of a father

The love of a single mother

The constant battle for cultural preservation

The failed relationships

The bridges we burned

The moments where we lost sense of

who we are

And after all that, we found each other

Confused by our dynamic

Yet accepting of the fact that

we're in each other's lives for a reason

Wondering about the purpose

And curious if we'll be friends forever or

Facebook friends with memories

We thought our obstacles were done and

yet the universe kept testing us

Only for the sake of having us discover and

understand the unconditional love we have for each other

Whether it's high up in the mountains

Or in the dry heat of the desert

Just know, we'll always have the stars

The Matriarch

I'm reminded of your faith

as I play gospel music every Sunday morning

Your energy when I seek to be the peacemaker

Your creativity when I season my food

Your guidance when I'm met with an obstacle

And your grace when I forgive myself when I have failed

I see you in times when

others give the last of what they have

to someone they don't even know

I hear you through negro spirituals and golden oldies

I feel you in the laughter of my sibling

And I understand you through the things

I've accomplished when others tried

to make me a statistic

9 years in flesh, yet forever in spirit

And your legacy still lives on

The granddaughter of a slave

The daughter of a survivor

The mother of a warrior

And the grandmother of a scholar

A love so unconditional

So passionate

Thicker than blood

And as red as a Ruby

Concussion

Your past created a labyrinth to your heart

I start at the beginning

I hit a fork on the pathway

Either I go left and face your insecurities

Or go right and face your doubts and trauma

I go left and hit a wall

Turned around and go down the other path

Surprise, I hit another wall

I attempt to forge my own path

Clawing through the thorny bushes of

memories of those who broke you

and betrayed your trust

My cunningness doesn't work for long

The labyrinth shifts into a different formation

I shift with it and am thrown against multiple barriers

Hard hits taken to the head

Trying to understand the maze of your cluttered thoughts

I meet some familiar faces along the new path to your heart

The unholy trinity themselves: Deflection, Silence, and Fear

Fear tries to scare me away

but I wrestle it into submission

I progress through the labyrinth

Silence observes me

and wonders why I'm even trying

We meet and have the ultimate stare down
Silence is simply an allusion in this maze
As I approach Silence with open arms
it questions my intentions
I get closer
Silence flinches
I get closer and say
there's nothing wrong with Silence
Silence looks at me
the spark reignited in its eyes
I hug Silence
Silence screams and cries tears of acceptance

Silence was created to act
as the ultimate line of defense
until I acknowledged how long
they've been screaming on the inside
this whole time
Silence lets me progress
Moving forward, I am met by Deflection
I see the light at the end of the maze
I'm so close to your heart
I hear the music it creates with its beat

Deflection shifts the maze
I keep moving

Deflection shifts the maze again

I keep moving

Deflection shifts the maze again

I'm lost

Deflection smirks with a maniacal gaze

I charge at Deflection head on

Deflection isn't used to straightforwardness

Nor were they ready for my blunt strikes

Each hit with the intent of understanding and grace

Deflection has been defeated

I move forward

I'm one step closer to your heart

Merely a few feet away, I'm stopped again

A wall of fire blocks the way to your heart

and from that fire emerges a lion

I don't know what to do

The lion charges at me

and swiftly strikes me with their paw

I'm unconscious

I wake up

I'm back at the start of the labyrinth

I'm sorry

I hope one day I can be good enough to make it to

your heart

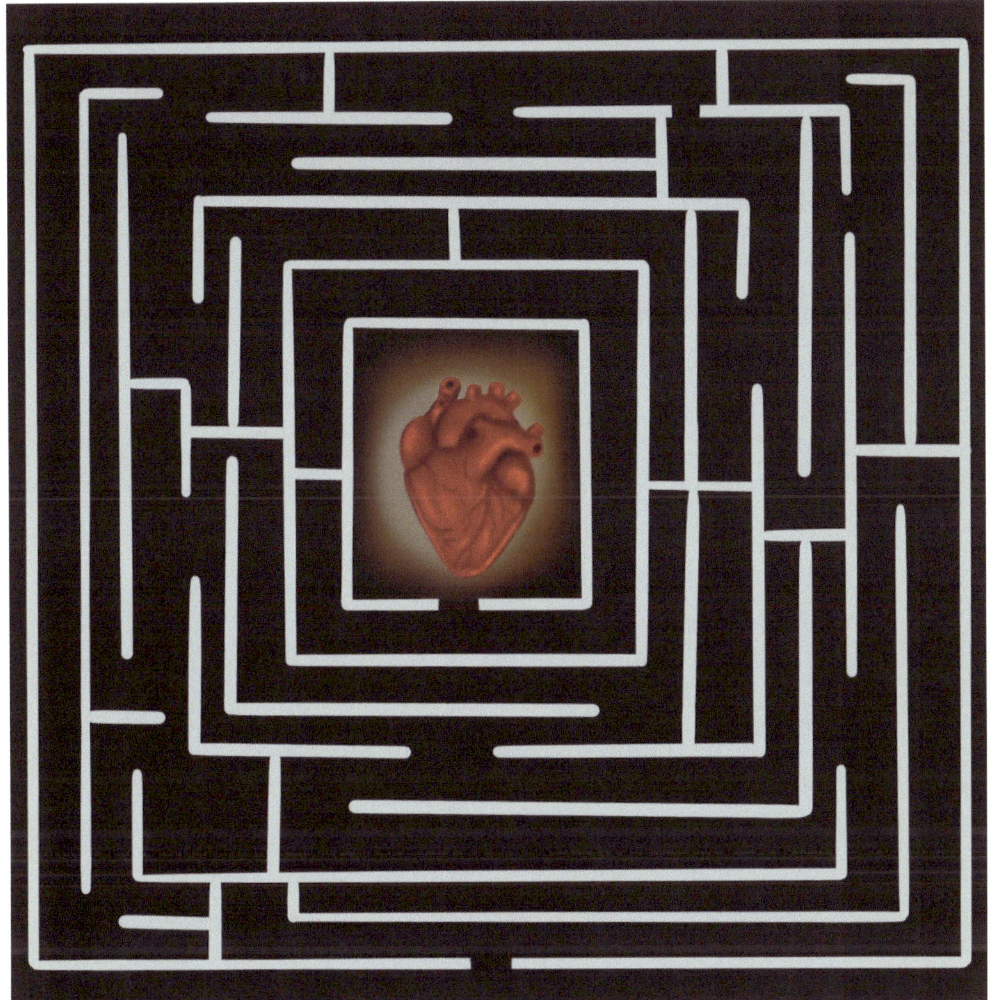

Jared

We found each other

I thought you were here for a visit

We met each other

I thought you were here for a reason

We got together

I thought you here for a lesson

We fell in love with each other

I thought you were here for a lifetime

You're still here

But not in that way

You're there for me

But not in that way

It's hard to love you

When it can't be in that way

MSY

Its insensitive to wish death on someone

Yet this being is a special exception

You know who you are and I wish you were gone

I wish you had never existed

You're very existence is intoxicating

The vision of your essence pains the pupils

Your aroma, rotten and rancid

I hate how easy it is for you to show up

The way you appear

In false promises

In toxic relationships

In hostile workplaces

In fake friendships

You arrive as someone new every time you visit

Wanting to top the damage you caused last time

I am amazed by your power

The fact that you can have others

follow your ways as if you're the deity

they've been needing to worship is astonishing

I don't get it

You use your energy

to give so much to people

and it's only to hurt them

To linger for a lifetime

To infect

To deceive

To break someone down so much

they forgot who they were

Your abilities, unmatched

Your presence, universal

Your origin story, different with each person

who mentions you in conversation

It's insensitive to wish death on someone

Yet this being is a special exception

You know who you are and I wish you were gone

I'm talking to you, Trauma

Life would be so much better

if you weren't alive and well

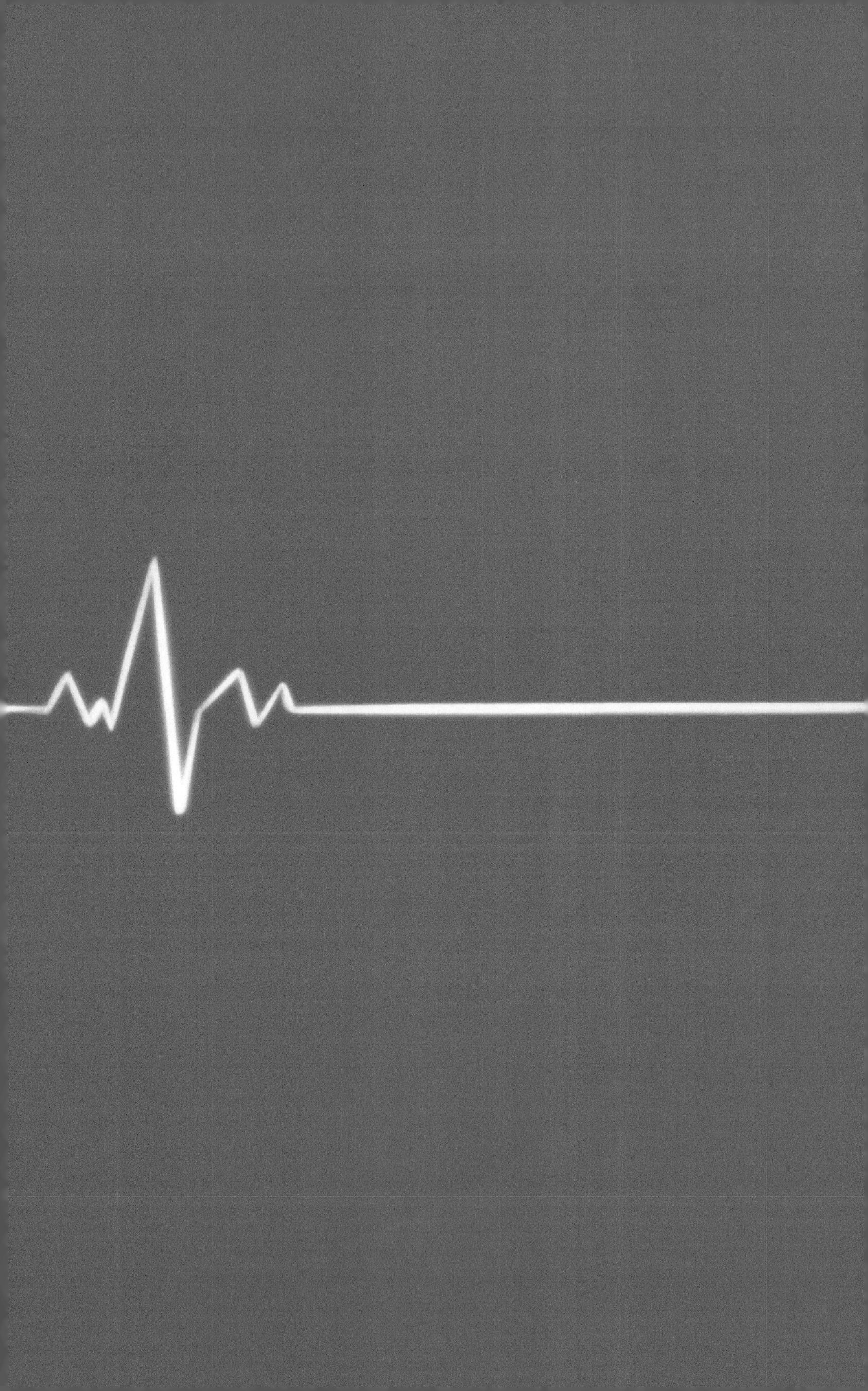

Creole Connection

I'm hanging on for dear life

to stay connected to you

Your legacy is my only lifeline

to our culture

To our people

To those who fought to keep our bloodline alive

9 years wasn't enough time

to learn from your teachings

I try to keep your memory alive

When I place a pan on the stove

Chop the vegetables

Mix the seasonings

Clean the rice

Pour the oil

Play the lowrider oldies

And pray

With hope I can recreate your kitchen

The other night I made your favorite dish

The one dish I never got to enjoy from you

Creole jambalaya

A pre-tarnished and unfulfilled soul

trying to make food that's good for it

I don't know our language

Living life to continue the legacy

without knowing the stories of our ancestors

Fighting to make it back to you

Back home

Dying to Live

Just because you dealt with a lot of clowns in your past

It doesn't mean your life has to run like a circus

In this day, we are choosing ourselves

We are making moves to achieve liberation and peace

Your points of reference are flawed but it's not your fault

Unfortunately...this world did a disservice to you

Like a tarnished necklace

You may be worn out and blemished

But it doesn't stop you from displaying your true beauty

and sentimental value

You may be broken like shattered glass

But instead of 7 years of bad luck

you're spending all 7 days of the week trying

to heal from the people who will never apologize

Love and healing may be priceless

But we need to acknowledge the true cost

where some of us will pay for someone else's mistakes

Much of your past was not within your control

But it does not define your future

For this time we've been given

This day

The present

will show us why we've been worthy enough to make it this far

Love and be loved

Heal and be healed

Manifest the disruption of trauma

And may you find peace

Cosmopolitan

Depression is the constant thought that

those who love you are frequently lying to you

because in reality, you're an inconvenience

The act of standing in an elevator

not knowing whether to go up or down

Listening to the same soundtrack of confusion

Afraid to get off because you feel safe

secluded from the world

Trying to breathe new life into what you lost

But because you're allergic to bullshit

not even Claritin can clear your airways

Wondering what life has in store for you

yet repeating that you didn't ask to be born

My god, it hurts to be human

Wanting to truly enjoy life,

but tired of playing the neverending game of

Russian roulette

Experiencing so much harm in this life

you mask yourself from the world before

COVID made you do it

And hoping all of this is just one big nightmare

Not wanting to be here

Yet the universe says you have to stay

Torn between wanting to know your purpose in life

and waiting for it to end at the same time

Rediscovery

Let's fall back in love with ourselves

The hustle and bustle of the city quickly makes time wither away

You greet me as your forever love and yet I treat you as a stranger

Reminiscing about the good old days when life seemed more lively

As a storm approaches, I listen to the gentle raindrops hit the concrete as they hit my face to blend in with my tears of forgotten memories

And for the first time in a long time, I'm reminded of how hard it is to be human

The rain keeps falling and I sit with the storm, the water and I sharing our memories

And I think of her

Her touch as gentle as warm blankets pulled from the dryer

Her grace as comforting as an embracing hug

Her curves to remind me of all the ups and downs we got through together

And her love of dance, where we both learned to love, lead, and follow

Like time, the storm eventually passes and I'm reminded of the love that never left my side

Here I am, ready to be us again

My love...may I have this dance?

WTF?

There was a time where I would stop the world for you

But then you stopped my world when you left

Now we sit here sending each other tik toks in silence

One Day Apart

I'm a spitting image of you
So similar, not even a mirror can show how much we're alike
I thought I could be you until I realized who you actually were
The very essence of your being made others shudder in dismay
Many of them afraid I'd follow the same path

I wanted you to try
To be there
To see my first moments
To bond
To teach
To love

The last time you saw me
You didn't even recognize me
Now I've come to terms with knowing
that the next time I see you is when you'll be buried
And when someone asks how I knew you
I can't say that I was your son
Even though I would really want to

189

Lakewood

Basking in the view of an October sunset

Yearning for my life to be as rich as the mountain air

My body, Still as the artist

My soul, at peace with the silence as the moon glistens over the red rock

Standing at a crossroads between who I am and who I need to be

For you

For them

For us

For me

Giving up a bit of myself before realizing my true worth

Mind more crowded than the downtown hustle

Carrying more baggage than the airport

Seeking a permanent vacation from reality

With hopes that you travel with me

Why I Run

As a kid, my friends and I would run anytime we heard police sirens

One day, we heard them, and of course, we ran

That day, the police officers caught up to us and asked "Why did you run?"

Personally, I couldn't give an answer

But now I have an answer...

I run to not be your statistic

Because you want me to run the path of your stereotypes

I run in the direction of opportunity

Because you want me to run in the direction of injustice

I run to not have my culture be painted as a monolith

Because you want it to run in unison as a community that can't succeed

I run for black men to go to places like Penn State

While you advocate for more of them to go to the state pen

I run for those black lives that were taken too soon

I run to prove I am not your negro, your hoodlum, or your coon

As a teenager, my friends and I would run anytime we heard police sirens

One day, we heard them, and of course, we ran

That day, the police officers caught up to us and asked "Why did you run?"

Personally, I couldn't give an answer

But things changed...

I was told to follow my dreams

But I run because I'm swiftly chasing them

For some of us, a dream is all we have

But I run to make those dreams a reality

You want me to run in a world that debates whether the glass is half empty or half full

But I choose to run in a world that addresses who's pouring the water

I run, I run, I run

I'm tired...

My mother told me life is not a bakery

But people still choose to sugarcoat the truth

Will I ever stop running?

As a kid, I ran out of fear

But times have changed

As an adult, why I run is more clear

I was expected to run to failure

I was expected to have it be the end of the chapter

But my story continued, because I kept running

My skills are now to a higher degree; masters

I used to run anytime I heard police sirens

One day, I heard them, but didn't run

The police officer told me "Thank you for not running, that means you're strong."

I told the police officer, "I'm done running, and besides, I've done nothing wrong."

I proudly walked away...

Aviata

Watching the sunset glisten the trees in the distance

The water swaying my body left and right

I'm surrounded by a vision of beauty that amazes me every time

I wonder what I did to deserve you

Yet accept the gift I've been given

As the sun sets, I find myself basking in your grace

When you're away for even just a second

I patiently wait for you to return so I can be happy again

Given Grace

Sitting in a warm room

With nothing but myself and my thoughts

The view of outside looks peaceful

But I know it's not because it's July in Vegas

It's interesting how even peace can be deceiving

Mistakes have been made

Regrets are still present

And yet, I try to give myself grace

A feeling that is temporary

A brief moment of peace

Seeing myself through a different lens

But being blind to my honest purpose in life

The grace withers away

The understanding departs from my soul

It's gone

I'm gonna miss this feeling that lets me be in love with myself

But...It doesn't have to end here

As the feeling was temporary

So can be it's absence

As I stand in the warm room with my thoughts

I do what is necessary so the heat doesn't suffocate me as much as my doubts

Walking to the window in my room to crack it open

A cool gentle breeze through a window on a hot summer day

That's what it feels like to give myself grace

The option but not the priority

You may be the person to show someone what they deserve

Even if you're not the person they're supposed to receive those things from

Sometimes, our role in other people's lives is to be the stepping stone instead of the final destination

To those who are still lost, I hope you accept and don't let go of what you really deserve

Response to TikTok Challenge

When I think of my mother

I think of light

A womxn so strong

She fought through love, trauma, and heartache to create me

A warrior conditioned to survive

A healer who filled your cup when hers was half empty

A teacher that the education system failed

A magician who could make a dollar out of 15 cents

A lover with a scarred heart

A boss that could make you disappear if you pissed her off

I think of family meetings to rejuvenate our love

My sister and I hoping for the best but preparing for the worst

A contagious laughter

And hugs so warm and welcoming

I got to forget about my troubles in the world

Just for a moment

I think of unconditional, yet conditional, but still unconditional love

With a constant reminder "I brought you into this world, and I'll take you out"

Mother-son dates to the mall

Where she'd spend the last of her money just to make sure I had shoes on my feet

The lessons of hard work, smart work, and heart work

The memory of when we had "The Talk"

And reminding me to keep my head held high

The constant reminder that I am no one's statistic, no one's sob story, and no one's nigger

The smell of Sunday dinner with Earth, Wind, and Fire blasting in the background

The food to remind us of history, our heritage, and our resilience

The neverending emails and text messages of resources and encouraging words of support for me and those around me

So loving that when you met her, you became her child

When I think of my mother

I am reminded of my purpose in this world

Entanglement Coffee

I'm here

I've always been here

For you

For the times you were doubtful

I was there

A phone call

A text

A DM

I was never leaving you

Too many others left you when it was inconvenient for them

I wanted to show you that it was never you that was the problem

I never left, I've always been here

Yet you kept me away

You placed me at a distance

Ashamed of your struggles and in fear of judgement

You handled it on your own and got through it

And here I stand because I've always been here

Waiting for you to understand

I never stopped caring

about you

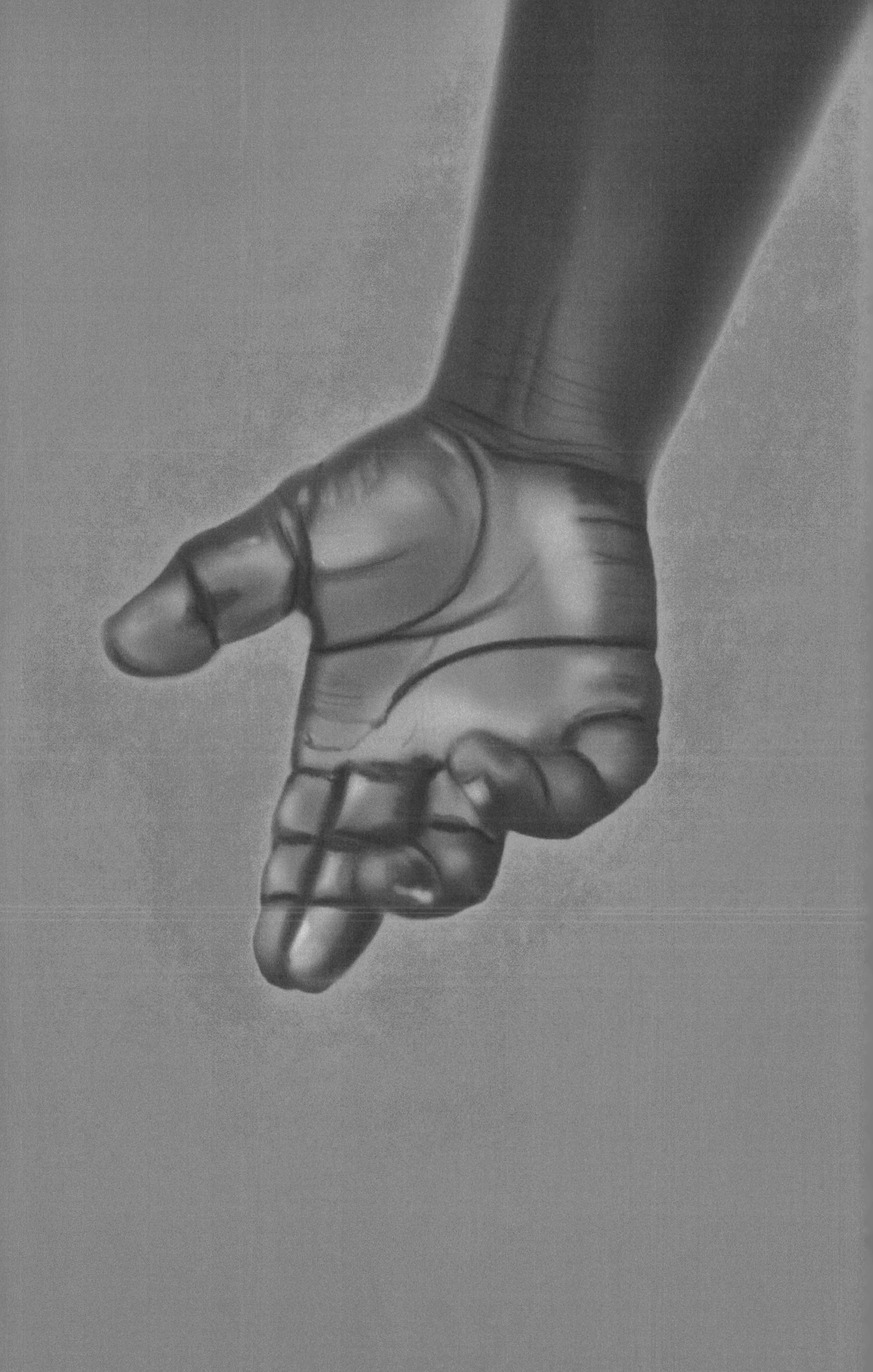

Fatherhood

I wanna have kids

But I also enjoy silence

Not sure if I wanna have them because they can distract me from the doubt in my mind

Or because I wanna have someone to die for

I come from the nation of fatherless men

And I'm clinching onto the fabric of hope to make this world a better place before I bring new life into it

I wanna look into the eyes of my child and tell them I love them

But I'm afraid this would be an aspect of life where I'm not welcomed, and am simply a trespasser

Pho

Whether it's a caress across your cheek

A tight hug you don't want to end

Or their fingers running through your hair

Don't take it for granted

A vision of beauty you get to see everyday

The live concert of them singing your favorite song

Moments of empowerment when you learn from them

Appreciate that

The delivery of your favorite food

Or having a conversation about that one show you can't stop obsessing over

For once, you're the priority

Having a constant feeling of bliss

Their very presence being the light of your world

Having your glow be noticed by others and it's because of their care

Cherish that love... always

December 16th

I thought I was meeting you for the first time

Instead, I was being reunited with someone I thought I'd never see again

I thought I was getting to know you

Instead you reminded me of who I was to you

We were closer than pieces of a puzzle

Yet personified yin and yang with our different personalities

I wanted to be with you and you felt the same

But we were worried about each other's safety due to circumstances

He didn't deserve you

And it pains me to know he was family

You were hurt and I had to sit front row to watch

You weren't loved and that's all I ever wanted to do to you, for you, and with you

Before my last breath, I told you

"Whatever happens, I'll see you in the next life"

Then we found each other

I was ecstatic to see you

And each day I'm not near you, I miss you more and more

You finally get to see me in a way you couldn't before

We no longer have the same limitations

We now have a chance to love each other in ways that were prohibited

No longer undercover

No longer keeping one of the longest standing secrets

You have me and now you're afraid to lose me

You knew you found me again

But had to get used to what I could offer because you were deprived of it in the past

I'm a lot to handle, and also a lot to lose

We're together, yet constantly fighting a figurative battle as if we will lose each other again

We found each other in this life

So let's do all that we can to build the life we deserve

I'm grateful to have you in this lifetime

And as I said before....whatever happens, I'll see you in the next life

Your Life

My journey into your life is defined by you

I may be in your life for a season

Or a lifetime

I may be in your life by accident

Or to give you a lesson

Either I'm the friend you always needed

Or maybe I'm the enemy you never knew existed

I could be your go-to person

Or I could be the "they" that brings you pain

I want to brighten your world when I enter it

Not when I leave it

If I truly am the villain in your story

Ask yourself what you did to make me that way

Villain
Hero

It hurts sometimes

Many people say to fear death

Yet death itself has breakfast with me every morning

We talk about sports, music, and sometimes even geek out on anime

The niceties dwindle after a few moments

We talk about who I'm going to lose next

Every time, I try to negotiate

"No! They have so much to live for, take me instead"

Death simply says "Not. Yet. You still have so much to do."

We laugh, we argue, I cry, and then death leaves

Then the cycle starts back over

I recall the memories of the one I lost

Looking for answers to questions I've asked 1000 times

Wondering why this is how things have to be

Struggling to function because it hurts to breathe

It hurts to walk

It hurts to move

And by staying alone in my bed, I'm safe

Waiting for my next meal with death

Gaslighting myself and hoping for good news

Huh?

Sometimes, I look in the mirror and hope my reflection

can give me answers I'm looking for

Then again, if my reflection is me

Then he is just as lost

Taking a deep dive into my soul to understand how I still have one

Confused by the thoughts racing in my head

Trying to speed to a singular thought only to be rear-ended or blindsided by another

I'm glad the world isn't a mirror

It's okay for others to see me in their own way

But I am afraid of them seeing me the way I see myself

GAOTU

It's easy for us to overlook simple visions of beauty

To know that your very existence started as an idea

Basking in the very glory of your being

To the great architect of the universe

I thank them for creating you

As you are a product of their vision

What's Next?

You were never expected

I didn't see you coming

And when I stumbled upon you

I felt as if we were meant to be together

I watched and observed you

Amazed and filled with wonder

I became obsessed with you

When I learned what you could give me

I pursued you

Others conditioned me to be suitable for you

I studied your every move

Then our worlds joined

And I soon realized we can't have a healthy relationship

Because of the lies you tell when I'm not around

Because of your history

Because of the company you keep

Because of the praise in public and the ridicule in private

I saw potential in you until I discovered your true colors

You call it politics, I call it politricks

You elevated me, but tried to make me assimilate

You said you appreciate me, but only acknowledge me 28 days a year

You surrounded me with others that look like me

Only for me to find out they're your side pieces and their character is already compromised

This toxic relationship is exhausting

And yet the only thing that keeps me here are the kids

I don't know when things will end between us

But just know....I can't do this anymore

JOKER

Sleepless Nights

The common explanation I tell people is that I'm a night owl

As the sun sets, I wonder what kind of night I'll have

7pm quickly turns to 11

11pm then turns to 2am

The usual suspects show up uninvited and unannounced

First we have insecurities

After they get comfortable, my inner demons come through

And then impostor syndrome shows up and they're the life of the party

Before I know it, all 3 trespassers are having a crump battle

Trying to decide who will have bragging rights and try to break me down

My mind races with thoughts I swore were buried

With trauma I swore reconciled

And with pain I swore I let go

Each night is a battle

And a complete toss up of whether I'll wake up rejuvenated or more tired

Then I lie to the world

"Hey Kevin, how are you?"

I'm fine

Take my anus

I once received an email that said:

"i loved you ivory. do you not want this tight hairy pink anus? YOU KNOW MINE IS TIGHTER THAN PAUL'S! I thought I was your little bitch!?"

I wish I was making this up

This is my job

To go through each day and simply experience ridiculousness

Let's talk about this email

The senders name is Jacob and y'all....Jacob needs a hug

A hug so tight, it's tighter than his anus

A hug so warm that he'll feel love he deserves but isn't getting from Ivory

Who knows? Maybe he needs to be with Ebony instead

To Ivory

What the fuck is going on?

It's one thing to play with someone's heart, but you've gone too far, you're playing with people's bootyholes

Wow....this just got deep, pun intended 😝

Ivory, just because you like dealing with shit sometimes doesn't mean you have to be a piece of shit yourself

Hurt people, hurt, people

Stop hurting Jacob, don't hurt Paul, and don't let this justify your own hurting

To Paul

Why are you here? Who are you? Clearly, you don't even go here

I pray you take time to reevaluate who has access to you

We done with that entanglement shit

Step your game up and keep your literal ass out of grown folks business

To all of you

When y'all get done messing with each other's asses

Take some time to look at a real moon

And ask yourself

Am I truly loved when my anus gets smashed

Or am I simply misconstruing that for the hole in my heart

Waiting to be filled?

The Visitor

Her heart is closed

Shuttered away in an empty room

4 blank walls

Confused about what to look forward to

I knock on the door

Her heart jumps

The locks get tighter

Constricted with failures and trauma from the past

I receive no answer

I tell her I'll come back tomorrow

I come back with good conversation and common interests

Her heart is curious of my intention

Concerned that my tongue will do nothing but provide a moment of woo
and false narratives

Here we are separated by a door that is the barrier to our joy

I get closer to the door

The locks tighten again

I apologize and say I'll come back tomorrow

I come back with food, humor, and a side of sarcasm

Her heart laughs hysterically

We hit it off and her heart decides to unlatch a few locks

The door is now cracked open

We make eye contact

We're both speechless

We experience our first touch

Her heart freezes, takes another look at me, and slams the door

I'm confused, I thought we were okay

I say I'll come back tomorrow

I come back with assurance, affirmation, and a moment to heal

Her heart is surprised

And yet, her heart wants this

I hope her heart will want this and me

The locks are gone

The door is open

But I'm still not welcome

I hope her heart will let me in

I wanna clean up the broken glass and create a new mirror so she can look at herself and love what she sees

I wanna exterminate the termites of her past trying to break down the strength of her foundation

I wanna kick out her toxic ass roommate impostor syndrome who's living rent free

I wanna sage her space to get rid of opinions, projections, and insecurities that tarnish her spirit

I wanna show her how we could make a home

But I'm afraid I'll just be nothing more than a visitor

Pandammit

The trouble in this world is so frequent

Some of us have never known peace

This pandemic sucks

Wear the damn mask

You may not get it, but some of us have been forced to wear a mask long before COVID

Gasping for a breath from the chokehold of bigotry and capitalistic destruction

Hiding half of our face as we hide much of ourselves because the world doesn't know how to love us

Being present each day when we would rather be absent and separated from others

We seize each day with the bare minimum

Not too much to be overglorified for our resilience

Not too little to leave this life behind

Just enough to simply exist

In time, our world will change again

This living hell will be over one day

And when that day comes, I'm excited for all of us to breathe again

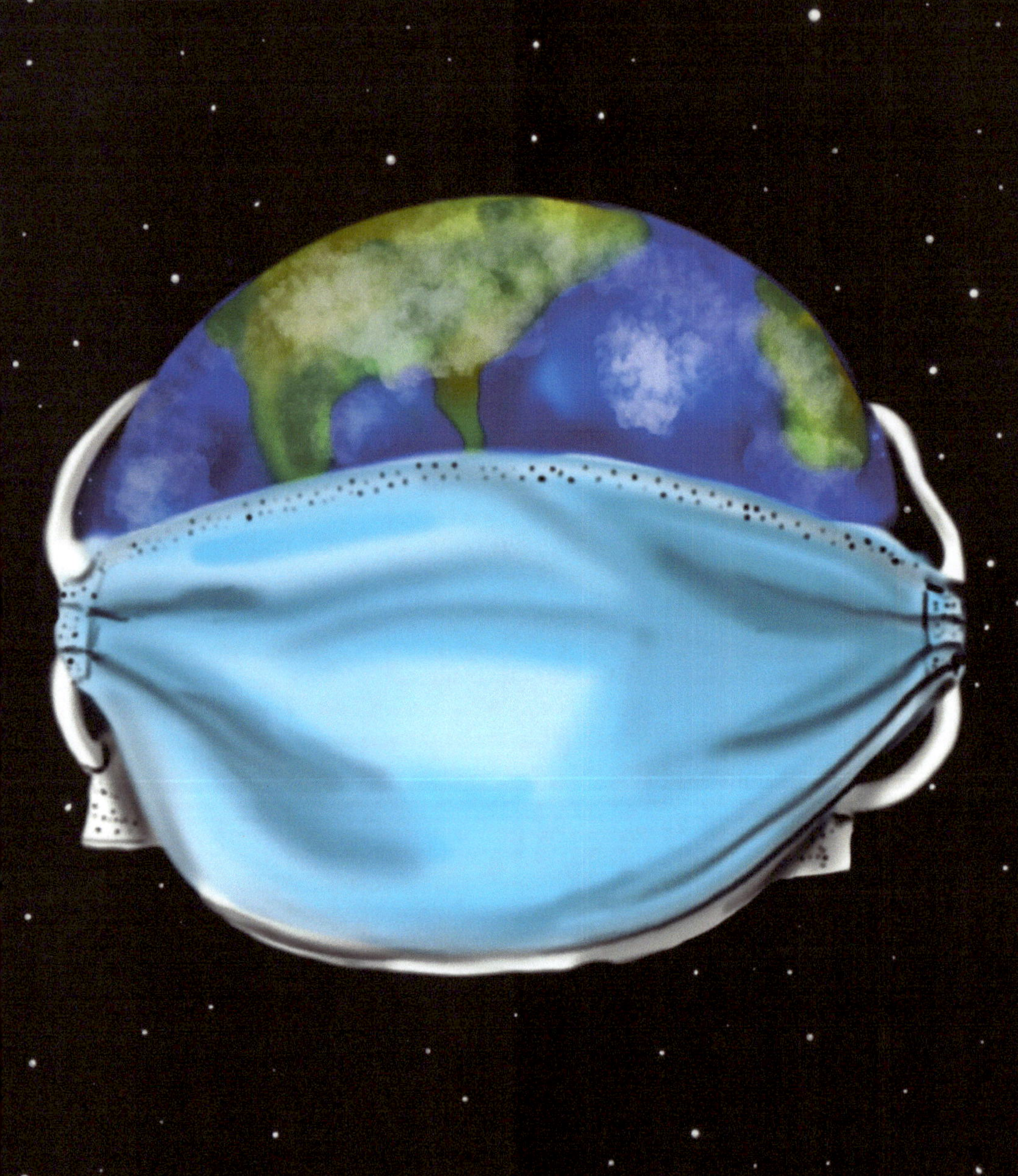

Blindsided

She saw me for everything I was and everything I am

She questioned

She challenged

She critiqued

She nagged

She cared

She embraced

She loved

Her last words were to not give up at the first sign of trouble

And then trouble took her away from me

I lived, I loved, and then a part of me died

Trying to fill that hole was like trying to hold water with tissue paper

Filled with the thought of being okay again

Filled with the desire to be loved again

Filled with the hope to love again

Chosen Family

Yeah, sex is cool and all

But have you ever hugged your best friend

And their embrace feels like home?

Their intentions, comforting

Their love, unconditional

Their vibe, unmatched

Their loyalty, sometimes stronger than blood

They bless us with their presence

And relieve us of our pain even when we don't ask

They make memories we'll never forget

And provide us with unpaid therapy

They deserve us at our best, but can also handle us at our worst

Our connection with them is not transactional

The way they complement our lives is a blessing in disguise

To my best friends, I thank you

I am a reflection of your love

And every moment with you is homecoming

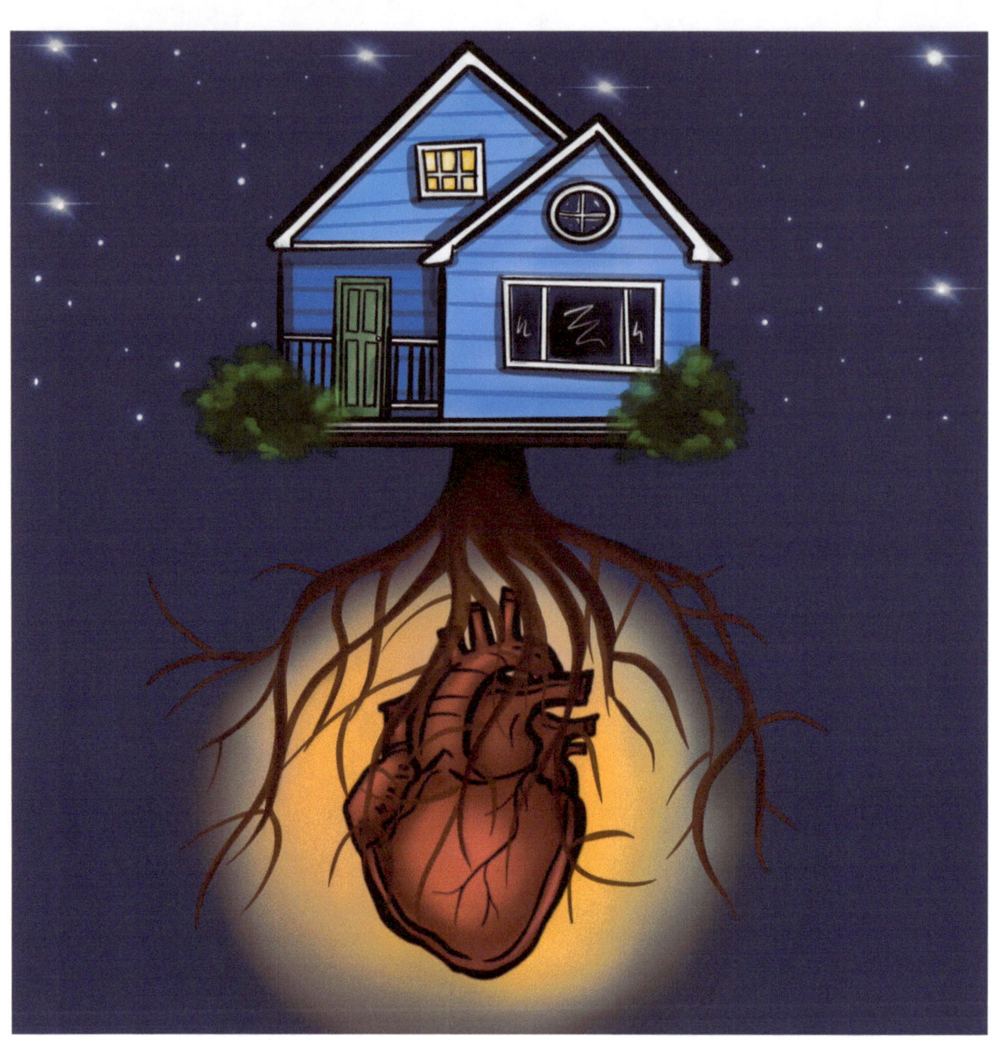

Summer Cleaning

Welcome back.

You've reclaimed your space. You were once caught up in the distractions of hardship

And may have been afraid of this world leaving you behind

Be proud of what you have taken back

For each artifact surrounding you is a reflection of your being

The art to honor your talents

The clothes to embrace your beauty

The plants to breathe new life

And the crystals to re-center your journey of enlightenment

You've trudged through a lot to get here

Be proud of where you're going

Rest and reflect, but don't get comfortable

Your truest reward is waiting for you

Mind Trip

Everytime you're not near me, I'm afraid I'm gonna lose you

Scared that you'll drift too far away

Confusing the suffocation of your dark thoughts as a warm embrace

Your mind is the battlefield and each insecurity is a new fight

Each time your mind wanders

All I ask is that you return

Come back and let us finish what we started

Come back to the love you were deprived of

Let my care serve as your map to journey your way back to healing

You've come so far

Don't let invalidation or unworthiness be the reason your former self re-emerges

Its okay to wander

Go ahead and explore where your mind takes you

Just don't lose yourself

Make it back

And when you return

I'll be waiting

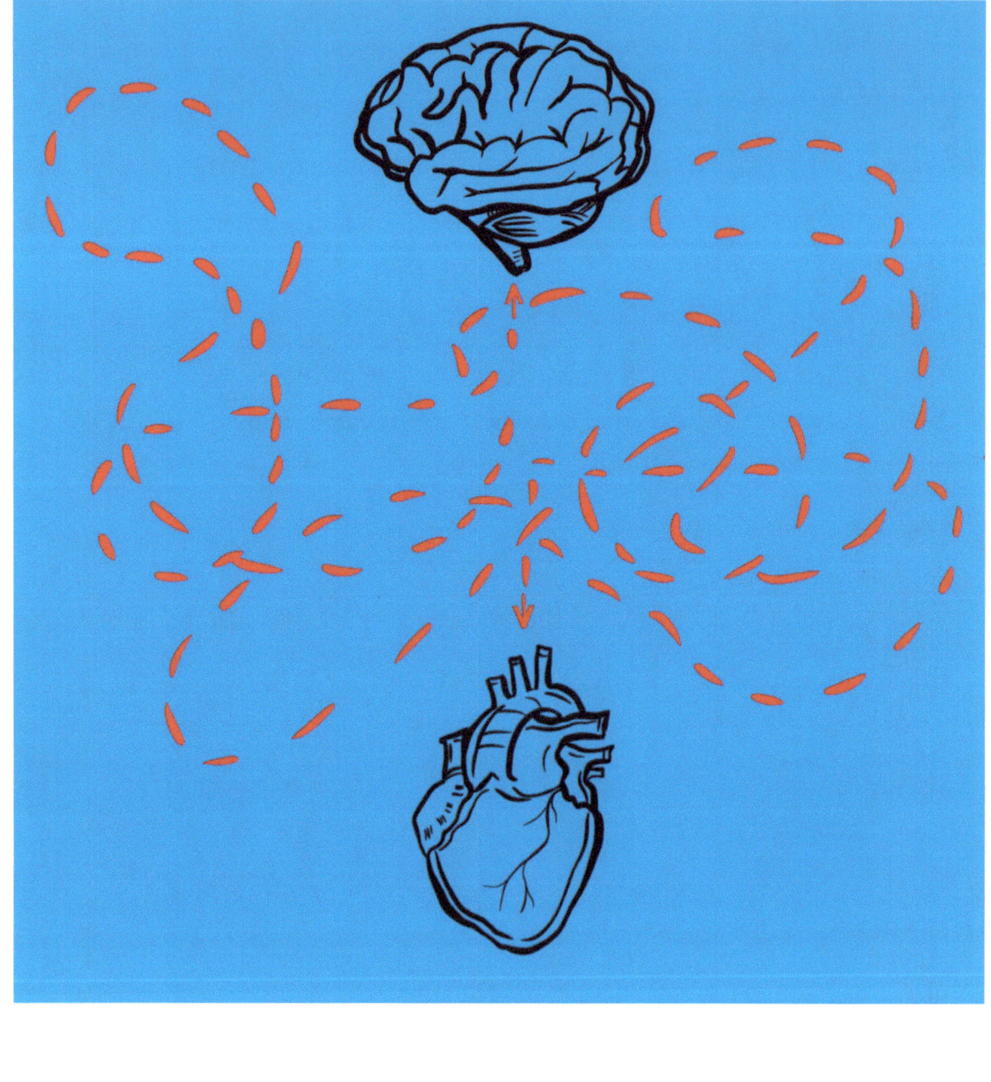

Heavy Degree

I wanted us all to come out on top

We came in as strangers in a cohort

Eventually, we became a family

13 dreams, 13 aspirations, 13 goals, and 13 different lives being lived

1 year later, 13 became 3

2 years later, 3 became just me

I'm called doctor now

To my cohort

My family

I know you're proud

And yet, I still feel guilty

University

Poolside

During peaceful nights

The sky is clear

Nature whispers

And my soul is still

Reflecting on whether I've been a blessing to this world

Or an inconvenience

Seeking to heal and be healed

Wanting to not cause harm

They say if you're not annoying, you're not paying attention

And as attentive as I am to the nuances of this world

It feels like I'm missing the things worth living for

Trying to live a life

And yet not knowing how to live it in the first place

Questioning whether the ones I love are ok with the fact that I was created

I don't know what I'm doing

But I hope it makes a difference

Galleria @ Sunset

Let's get to the point

I'm big

I'm a man of size

I'm thicc with 2 C's

I'm curvy

I'm fat

And I love myself

Yesterday, I went to the mall

A place that's mainly a miss for the big folx

I walk from store to store, where I'm constantly reminded of fatphobia and capitalism

A womxn claws through the clothes, desperate for one piece to match her stature

Unfortunately she falls victim to the sign that's gaslighting her: big and tall

We lock eyes, and realize we are surrounded by lies bound together by fabricated styles and well-intentioned staff

She eventually accepts her disappointment, hugs me tight, and reflects on how she has never fit in this world

We leave and go to the only part of the mall that accepts us: the food court

Backs hunched over, elbows deep on the edge of the table, heads heavy and hanging down

Time goes by and I'm able to cheer her up

We leave the mall

As she walks away, she shares she has hope for a better day

I pray she finds peace, for it is not only her body that's big in this world, but also her heart

To my students

Your light blinded me

Your curiosity made me laugh

And your sass pissed me off

"Mr Wright, I need this"

"Hey Kevin, could you please do me a favor?"

While I rolled my eyes when your requests were last minute

I still did what I could to help you

I saw you all the time

But that stopped

Like an eclipse, I would only see you if I was in the right place at the right time

Then I stopped seeing you

My phone rang

I answered

I received the news no one likes to hear

You were gone

I fought for you

And now I fight to keep your memory alive

I invested in you

And now I invest hundreds of dollars in counseling

I love you

And now I hope you love where the next life has taken you

To those who are listening

How do you know when someone is proud of you when they're not here
to tell you?

Loving Day

My goal is to put a smile on your face

To receive and be comforted by your grace

With each day that passes, you're the last sight I want to see

It took a lot for us to get here and beside you is where I wanna be

I'm here to fight every battle - your doubts, fears, and insecurities

So that one day you see the beauty in yourself, and push out all that negativity

In the past, our love was considered illegal

In the present, our love is hated by ignorant people

There will be many obstacles to keep love like ours apart

We're ready, ride or die, its been like that from the very start

I know you may be scared of where things may go

Let me be there to show you how much our love can grow

The universe brought us together for a reason

I'm here for a lifetime, not just a season

You received pain and harm from others who didn't know how to love

I'm here to show you the love that you're worthy of

Have faith in us, trust in me, fulfill your desire

What we have isn't just a relationship, it's surefire

Productive Night

The artist wakes up everyday and paints their dreams into a reality

They carve complex thoughts into masterpieces

An empty canvas is not blank to them, but instead filled with opportunity

Pure and unfiltered expression is their love language

The teacher sleeps each night trying to sort out thousands of thoughts

They share the wisdom of our ancestors

An empty mind is their biggest foe, yet a reminder that knowledge ebbs and flows

Their priority is to help us learn from mistakes of the past

The artist and teacher may not see eye to eye

Their worlds may be different, and yet they both serve a greater purpose

The artist honors our ancestors teachings through their creation

The teacher sculpts the minds of others to grow into walking masterpieces

Both have enlightened our peers

Both have changed our world

For the artist, their canvas is their classroom

For the teacher, their students are future works of art

I am yearning to learn from both

Juneteenth

My favorite magicians are Black people

Creating maps with our hair

Telling stories with our quilts

Navigating on stolen land with the stars

Communicating with the clap of our hands or stomps with our feet

Surviving over 20 massacres

Creating almost every popular genre of music

Building a whole country after being stolen from a continent

Having miracles happen with little to nothing

And that's just act one

Breaking out of shackles when no one would give us the key

Fighting for one man's dream and doing so by any means necessary

From building the White House to running the White House

You can't tell me Black people aren't magical

However not all magic is good

While our presence may leave people in shock and awe

The real trick is the slight of hand our nation is controlling

Pointing to how we no longer have a racism issue

When really, we haven't revealed the illusion

Knowledge

12 years of preparation for the SAT and ACT

Working hard not knowing if I'm getting the diploma or a GED

Fighting through the bullshit to get a degree

4 years of preparation for the GRE just to get another degree

3 more years to earn the EdD just to end up with PDD

Post doctoral depression is real

And yet our credentials create the illusion that being educated means being stable when not everyone understands what it took to get there

It is a privilege to be my ancestors wildest dream and at the same time, I'm angry with the nightmares of failure that occurred during this journey

I'm resilient; displaced, but not defeated

My mental health: unstable and depleting

Grateful to epitomize Black excellence

Yet saddened by the collateral damage

Stuck in limbo, questioning what's heavier

The degree or the crown?

Is this real?

I wake up with joy and for once, it's not synthetic

To reconcile the troubles of my past

Letting go of what was and now accepting what is

Building a life anew and actually having control

When I gaze, I see into the world with positive light

Hoping to shine onto others

No longer desperate for acceptance and love

It was never good enough from others because I never gave it to myself

Trauma consumed most of my life before I realized I could let it go

I kept confusing healing for heartache

Comfort for complacency

And love for lies

Sometimes I wonder if all of this is a dream

Have I truly healed?

Or have I simply mastered the art of gaslighting?

That way of thinking will no longer control me

I'm here

I'm thriving

My heart and soul are finally one

Heal

It's amazing right?

To heal and be healed with love

And you deserve it

Thank You

Dear Reader,

First and foremost, thank you for buying this book. It is an honor to know you took the time to invest in my work. The journey from ghostwriting to actually publishing poetry with my name on it was a wild ride. However, it has been worth it every step of the way because of people like you. My healing journey is not complete just yet, but this book is a huge step that was able to have me achieve so much progress. You probably noticed that each piece was from a different era of my life; some have provided closure, while some still require more Heart Work. You may have also raised an eyebrow once or twice when looking at the artwork attached to each poem. That's okay, and I am more than happy to connect and hear your interpretations of each poem and piece of artwork. You can connect with me in the following ways:

Instagram: @k_wright92

Twitter/X: @k_wright92

I appreciate your care and support so much!

In Solidarity,
Kevin L. Wright